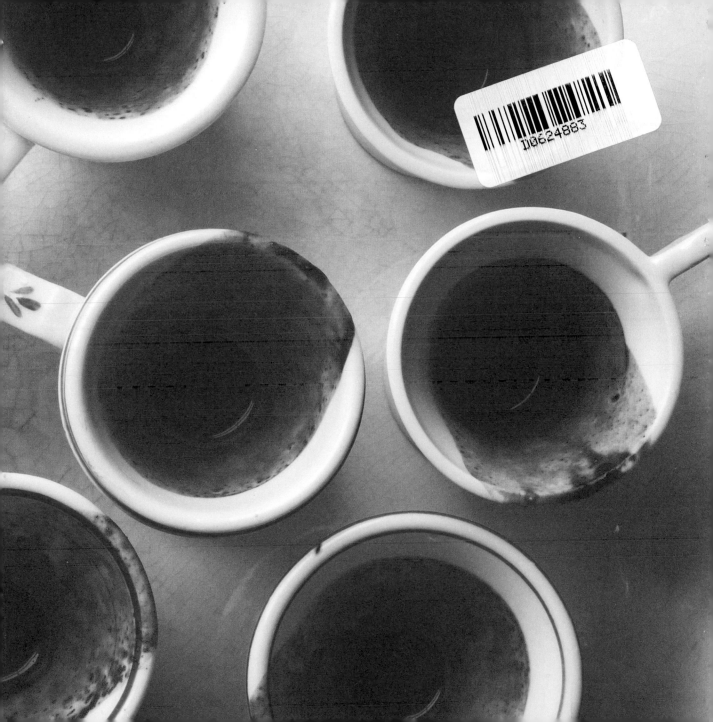

Hot Chocolate

Hot Chocolate

RYLAND PETERS & SMALL
LONDON • NEW YORK

Hannah Miles

photography by Steve Painter

For my special nephew Bowen xxx

DESIGN, PHOTOGRAPHY AND PROP STYLING Steve Painter
EDITOR Kate Eddison
HEAD OF PRODUCTION Patricia Harrington
ART DIRECTOR Leslie Harrington
EDITORIAL DIRECTOR Julia Charles
PUBLISHER Cindy Richards

FOOD STYLIST Lucy McKelvie
INDEXER Hilary Bird

First published in 2015 by
Ryland Peters & Small
20–21 Jockey's Fields
London WC1R 4BW
and
341 E 116th St
New York NY 10029

www.rylandpeters.com

10 9 8 7 6 5 4 3 2

Text © Hannah Miles 2015
Design and photographs © Ryland Peters & Small 2015

Printed in China

ISBN: 978-1-84975-659-4

A CIP record for this book is available from the British Library.
US Library of Congress CIP data has been applied for.

NOTES
· All spoon measurements are level unless otherwise specified.
· All eggs are medium (UK) or large (US), unless otherwise specified.
Uncooked or partially cooked eggs should not be served to the very
old, frail, young children, pregnant women or those with
compromised immune systems.
· When a recipe calls for the grated zest of citrus fruit, buy unwaxed
fruit and wash well before using. If you can only find treated fruit,
scrub well in warm soapy water before using.

Contents

Introduction

When days are cold and chilly and you are in need of a warming treat, there is nothing nicer than a steaming mug of creamy hot chocolate, especially when topped with luxurious whipped cream or delicious melting marshmallows.

Hot chocolate is one of the oldest drinks known to man, perfected by the Mayas and Aztecs thousands of years ago. Originally made from pounding cocoa pods/beans with spices and water and then heating it, hot chocolate has always been popular.

Over the years it has spread throughout the world with classic versions in all countries – Italians drink 'cioccolata densa' that is so thick that you can almost stand a spoon up in it. Viennese hot chocolate, thickened with egg yolk, is one of my favourites, while in America the most popular hot chocolate is thinner and made with cocoa powder.

While there are a wide variety of hot chocolate powders available in the supermarket, there is nothing nicer than making your own hot chocolate from scratch. The recipes in this book use all types of chocolate – white, milk and plain/semisweet chocolate are blended to make all your favourite flavour combinations.

This book contains 28 delectable recipes inspired by countries all around the world. For those of you who like pure and simple hot chocolate, the World Classics chapter contains French vanilla hot chocolate, an indulgent mocha and chocolat L'Africain - thick, luxurious chocolate 'custard' inspired by Angelina's in Paris.

Candy bars are perfect for making quirky sweet drinks, and the Candy and Cakes chapter contains delicious recipes for such delights as toffee apple hot chocolate, malted hot chocolate topped with crunchy chocolate malt balls and the all-American favourite s'mores hot chocolate with marshmallows on top and digestive biscuit/graham cracker crumbs coating the rim of your glass.

In Fireside Favourites you will find warming drinks with hints of spices and many with a boozy kick. This chapter includes my favourite, la bomba – I spent many happy evenings drinking this hot chocolate in Mallorca. Alternatively, why not try an Indian chai-spiced white hot chocolate infused with the warming flavours of cardamom, cinnamon and nutmeg?

Finally when it comes to the holiday season and you have guests staying over, why not treat them to recipes from the Festive Treats chapter, which contains winter-themed hot chocolates such as gingerbread-spiced, eggnog and peppermint candy cane hot chocolate.

Whatever type of chocolate is your guilty pleasure, from the creamiest white chocolate to dark/bittersweet, there are warming drinks a-plenty in this delightful little book.

World classics

French vanilla hot chocolate

This is a classic hot chocolate made with white chocolate and vanilla. Topped with indulgent marshmallow fluff and pretty green pistachios, this is one of my favourite drinks. As this hot chocolate is rich, it is best made with skimmed milk, although you can substitute whole/full-fat milk or even a combination of milk and cream, if you prefer.

1 vanilla pod/bean
500 ml/2 cups skimmed milk
100 g/3½ oz. white chocolate, chopped
2 heaped tablespoons marshmallow fluff
finely chopped pistachios, to sprinkle

Serves 2

Split the vanilla pod/bean in half lengthways and scrape out the seeds by running the back of the knife along each half of the pod/bean.

Place the milk, chopped chocolate, vanilla seeds and scraped pod/bean in a saucepan over low heat and simmer until the chocolate has melted, whisking all the time.

Pour into two cups and top each with a large spoonful of marshmallow fluff. Sprinkle with chopped pistachios and serve immediately.

Viennese hot chocolate

For cake and hot chocolate lovers, Vienna is the place to visit. I spent a weekend there a few years ago with my friend Maren, and we drank more hot chocolate in 48 hours than I ever dreamed possible. My favourite cafe, Demel, serves the classic Austrian hot chocolate and this is my interpretation of that luxurious drink.

125 ml/½ cup milk

125 ml/½ cup double/heavy cream

100 g/3½ oz. dark/bittersweet chocolate (minimum 70% cocoa solids), chopped

1 tablespoon granulated/white sugar

1 egg yolk, whisked

Serves 2

Place the milk and cream in a saucepan with the chopped chocolate and sugar. Place over low heat and whisk until the chocolate has melted and the drink is thick and syrupy.

Remove the pan from the heat and allow to cool for a few minutes, then beat in the whisked egg yolk to thicken the hot chocolate.

Return to the heat, whisking all the time, until hot. Pass through a sieve/strainer and then pour into two cups and serve straight away.

Chocolat l'Africain

Nestled on the Rue de Rivoli in Paris is a patisserie/tea room like no other – Angelina's. It is always top of my list when visiting the French capital. In addition to delectable cakes, they serve hot chocolate that is quite honestly to die for. This is my make-at-home version for times when you need to indulge yourself but can't spare the time to travel to Paris!

250 ml/1 cup milk

200 ml/generous ¾ cup double/heavy cream

100 g/3½ oz. dark/bittersweet chocolate (85% cocoa solids), chopped

2 tablespoons icing/confectioners' sugar, sifted

½ teaspoon ground cocoa nibs (optional)

a pinch of vanilla bean powder or ½ teaspoon pure vanilla extract

Serves 2

Place the milk and 50 ml/3 tablespoons of the cream in a saucepan with the chopped chocolate, 1 tablespoon of the icing/confectioners' sugar and the ground cocoa nibs. Whisk over low heat until the chocolate has melted and the drink is thick and syrupy.

I like to leave the cocoa nibs in the drink, but if you prefer smooth hot chocolate, pass the drink through a fine-mesh sieve/strainer.

To prepare the Chantilly cream to serve on top of the hot chocolate, place the remaining cream in a bowl with the remaining 1 tablespoon of sifted icing/confectioners' sugar and the vanilla bean powder or extract, and whisk to soft peaks.

Pour the hot chocolate into two cups and serve straight away with cream on the side ready to spoon on top.

If you prefer a less sweet hot chocolate, you can omit the icing/confectioners' sugar from the cream.

Italian cioccolata densa

This classic Italian hot chocolate is so thick that you can almost stand a spoon up in it! Think part hot chocolate, part chocolate ganache. It is rich and indulgent, so you only need to serve it in the smallest of cups. I love to serve it with little Italian cookies, such as ricciarelli or pignoli on the side for dipping, or why not serve it instead of dessert?

2 teaspoons cornflour/
cornstarch, sifted

200 ml/generous ¾ cup milk

100 g/3½ oz. plain/semisweet
chocolate, chopped

200 ml/generous ¾ cup
double/heavy cream

1 tablespoon icing/
confectioners' sugar

Serves 2

Whisk the cornflour/cornstarch with a little of the milk until it is a smooth paste and has no lumps. Set aside.

Place the chopped chocolate in a saucepan with the remaining milk and the cream. Place over low heat and simmer until the chocolate has melted, whisking all the time.

Add the icing/confectioners' sugar and cornflour/cornstarch mixture to the pan and whisk in. Heat gently until the hot chocolate becomes very thick, whisking all the time. If there are any lumps, pass the mixture through a fine-mesh sieve/strainer before serving.

Pour the hot chocolate into two cups and serve immediately with spoons.

Salted caramel white hot chocolate

This is an intensely creamy hot chocolate with a rich caramel flavour – perfect for a cold winter day. For an extra-special effect, pipe caramel swirls into your glasses to serve, which provide a perfect contrasting pattern to the golden drink. I prefer to use skimmed milk in this recipe, rather than a combination of milk and cream, otherwise the drink can be a little too rich since it has cream on top. However, if you are after a truly decadent drink you can replace some of the milk with cream. If you can only find caramel sauce or toffee sauce, simply add a pinch of salt to the milk.

4 tablespoons salted caramel sauce

100 g/3½ oz. white chocolate, chopped

500 ml/2 cups skimmed milk

200 ml/generous ¾ cup double/heavy cream

piping/pastry bag fitted with a small round nozzle/tip

piping/pastry bag fitted with a large star nozzle/tip

Serves 2

Place 1 tablespoon of the caramel sauce into the piping/pastry bag fitted with the small round nozzle/tip and pipe decorative swirls inside two tall, heatproof glasses. Set aside until you are ready to serve, reserving some of the caramel sauce in the piping bag for decoration.

Place the chopped white chocolate in a saucepan with the milk and 2 tablespoons of the caramel sauce. Heat gently over low heat until the chocolate has melted, whisking all the time. Remove the hot chocolate from the heat.

Place the cream in a bowl with the final tablespoon of caramel sauce and whisk to stiff peaks. Spoon the cream into the piping/pastry bag fitted with the large star nozzle/tip.

Heat the hot chocolate again gently and carefully pour into the prepared glasses. Pipe a swirl of caramel cream on top of each glass and drizzle with a little of the reserved caramel. Serve immediately.

Mocha

When you need an intense buzz of caffeine, this is the hot chocolate for you. A thick, indulgent hot chocolate served with a shot of espresso coffee on the side and a rich coffee cream, allowing you to blend the chocolate, coffee and cream to your own taste. This is the ultimate morning wake-up call.

250 ml/1 cup milk

100 g/3½ oz. dark/bittersweet chocolate (85% cocoa solids), chopped

2 tablespoons icing/confectioners' sugar, sifted

125 ml/½ cup double/heavy cream

1 teaspoon coffee extract

2 shots hot espresso coffee

Serves 2

Place the milk in a saucepan with the chopped chocolate and 1 tablespoon of the icing/confectioners' sugar and whisk over low heat until the chocolate has melted and the drink is thick and syrupy.

To prepare the coffee cream to serve on top, place the cream in a bowl with the coffee extract and remaining icing/confectioners' sugar, and whisk to soft peaks.

To serve, pour the hot chocolate into little jugs, and serve alongside the hot espressos and the coffee cream. Your guests can then blend the hot chocolate and espresso together themselves in such quantities as they wish, with a large spoonful of coffee cream on top.

Sea salt chocolate

This deliciously thick hot chocolate is the perfect combination of sweet and salty. You can make this hot chocolate with milk, white or dark/bittersweet chocolate and adjust the salt to your own taste. For a salted caramel hot chocolate, use caramel chocolate such as Caramac for a rich alternative, or why not add a spoonful of salted caramel sauce to the pan with the milk in addition to the chocolate? Serve with biscotti to dip into the hot chocolate.

250 ml/1 cup milk

250 ml/1 cup double/heavy cream

100 g/3½ oz. dark/bittersweet chocolate (70% cocoa solids), chopped

1 tablespoon caster/granulated sugar

½ teaspoon salt (or to taste)

1 egg yolk

Serves 2

Place the milk, cream and chopped chocolate in a saucepan with the sugar and salt, and heat over low heat until the chocolate has melted, whisking all the time.

Taste to see whether you need to add a little more salt for an extra salty kick. Remove from the heat and whisk in the egg yolk to thicken the hot chocolate.

Pass it through a sieve/strainer, then pour into two cups and serve immediately.

Candy and cakes

Malted hot chocolate

Malted drinks are some of the most comforting and this hot chocolate is what I love to drink when I am in need of a hug in a mug. I like to include lots of malt powder, so that the hot chocolate is thick and syrupy, although you can add a little less if you prefer thinner hot chocolate. Top with whipped cream and malted chocolate balls for an extra-special treat.

100 g/3½ oz. milk chocolate, chopped

250 ml/1 cup milk

450 ml/1¾ cups double/heavy cream

3 tablespoons malted drink powder (such as Horlicks or Ovaltine)

chocolate malt balls (such as Maltesers or Whoppers), chopped

Serves 2

Place the chopped chocolate in a heatproof bowl over a pan of simmering water and heat gently over low heat until melted.

Place the milk and 250 ml/1 cup of the cream in a saucepan and bring gently to the boil. Add the melted chocolate to the pan with the malted drink powder and simmer over low heat until the chocolate is combined, whisking all the time. Pour the hot chocolate into two cups.

Whip the remaining cream to stiff peaks and place a large spoonful on top of each drink. Sprinkle with the crushed malt balls and serve straight away.

Coconut hot chocolate

This hot chocolate is laced with rum and coconut cream – perfect for a taste of the tropics when it is chilly outside. I like to serve toasted long shredded coconut on top for decoration. Omit the rum if serving to children.

1 tablespoon long shredded coconut

100 g/3½ oz. milk chocolate, chopped

250 ml/1 cup milk

250 ml/1 cup double/heavy cream

160 ml/scant ⅔ cup coconut cream

5 tablespoons coconut rum

spray cream, or double/heavy cream, whipped to stiff peaks, for topping

Serves 2

Begin by toasting the coconut in a dry frying pan/skillet, stirring all the time until it is golden brown. Take care as the coconut can burn easily. As soon as it starts to turn lightly golden brown, tip it out onto a plate. If you leave it in the hot pan it will continue to cook and may burn.

Place the chopped chocolate in a heatproof bowl over a pan of simmering water and heat gently until melted.

Spoon the melted chocolate into a saucepan with the milk, cream and coconut cream and bring gently to the boil, whisking all the time. Remove from the heat and add the coconut rum. (Adding it after removing it from the heat means that you will not burn off the alcohol.)

Pour the hot chocolate into two cups. Top with spray or whipped cream and decorate with the toasted coconut. Serve immediately.

Boston cream

I served this recipe to my friend Poppy (aged 11) who, with marshmallow fluff on her nose, chin and all around her mouth, declared that it was delicious. The vanilla-scented hot chocolate is topped with a marshmallow layer and then decorated with a chocolate spiral inspired by the popular American cake Boston cream pie.

150 g/5½ oz. milk chocolate, chopped

250 ml/1 cup milk

1 teaspoon vanilla bean paste or pure vanilla extract

2 heaped tablespoons marshmallow fluff

piping/pastry bag fitted with a small round nozzle/tip

Serves 2

Place the chopped chocolate in a heatproof bowl over a pan of simmering water and heat gently until the chocolate has melted. Remove from the heat and add two-thirds of the chocolate to a saucepan with the milk and vanilla.

Whisk over low heat until the chocolate has blended with the milk and the drink is hot.

Divide the hot chocolate between two cups. Place a large spoonful of marshmallow fluff on top of each cup and leave for a few minutes until the marshmallow begins to melt, then spread out over the surface of the drinks to make an even layer.

Spoon the reserved melted chocolate into the piping/pastry bag and pipe a tight spiral of chocolate on top of the marshmallow, starting at the centre.

Using a sharp knife, pull a line from the centre of the marshmallow to the edge of the cup to make a feathered pattern with the chocolate, and repeat all the way round the cup so that you end up with a completely feathered spiral. Serve immediately.

Red velvet hot chocolate

This hot chocolate is inspired by the popular American red velvet cake, which is traditionally made with cocoa powder and red food colouring. The same ingredients are used in this hot chocolate and, for extra fun, each serving is topped with a scoop of ice cream so you can enjoy the hot/cold sensation as you drink this treat. If you are serving this with a red velvet cake, sprinkle a few crumbs on top to decorate. If you don't have a red velvet cake to hand, use some sugar sprinkles instead.

500 ml/2 cups milk

100 g/3½ oz. milk chocolate, chopped

1 tablespoon unsweetened cocoa powder, sifted

a few drops of red food colouring

2 scoops of vanilla ice cream

red velvet cake crumbs or sugar sprinkles, to decorate

ice cream scoop

Serves 2

Place the milk and chopped chocolate in a saucepan with the cocoa powder and heat over low heat until the chocolate has melted and the cocoa is incorporated, whisking constantly.

Add a few drops of red food colouring to give the drink a nice reddish brown colour.

Pour the hot chocolate into two cups, place a scoop of ice cream on top of each and decorate with cake crumbs or sugar sprinkles. Serve immediately with spoons to eat the ice cream.

S'mores hot chocolate

S'mores are a delicious campside treat popular all over America – toasted marshmallows and chocolate are sandwiched between graham crackers or digestive biscuits. That delicious snack is the inspiration for this fun and warming drink. You will need a chef's blow torch for this recipe.

100 g/3½ oz. milk chocolate, chopped

2 graham crackers or digestive biscuits

250 ml/1 cup milk

250 ml/1 cup double/heavy cream

2 giant marshmallows

chef's blow torch

Serves 2

Begin by preparing two heatproof glasses. Place the chopped chocolate in a heatproof bowl over a pan of simmering water and heat over low heat until melted. Carefully dip the rims of each glass into the chocolate.

Crush the graham crackers or digestive biscuits by placing them in a clean plastic bag and bashing them with a rolling pin. Place the crumbs on a plate and dip the chocolate-coated rim of each glass in the crumbs to decorate. Set aside until you are ready to serve.

Spoon the remaining melted chocolate into a saucepan with the milk and cream, and heat over low heat, whisking all the time. Pour the hot chocolate into the prepared glasses, taking care not to pour over the chocolate-crumb rim decoration.

Place each marshmallow on a toasting fork and toast with the blow torch to caramelize. Take care not to burn the marshmallows. While the marshmallows are still warm, place one on top of each glass. Serve immediately.

Turkish delight hot chocolate

This hot chocolate tastes of the Orient with hints of rose and Turkish delight. Topped either with chunks of Turkish delight or elegant edible rose petals, this is a drink to serve to people you love. It is rich and indulgent, made with dark/bittersweet chocolate, so sweeten with sugar to your taste.

100 g/3½ oz. dark/bittersweet chocolate (85% cocoa solids), chopped

350 ml/1½ cups milk

350 ml/1½ cups double/heavy cream

1 tablespoon caster/granulated sugar

2 teaspoons rose extract or rose syrup

4 cubes of mixed pink and red Turkish delight

edible rose petals, to decorate (optional)

piping/pastry bag fitted with a large star nozzle/tip

Serves 2

Place the chopped chocolate in a saucepan with the milk, 150 ml/⅔ cup of the cream, the sugar and 1 teaspoon of the rose extract or syrup. Heat gently over low heat until the chocolate and sugar have melted, whisking all the time. Remove the hot chocolate from the heat while you prepare the cream topping.

Place the remaining cream in a bowl with the final teaspoon of rose extract or syrup and whisk to stiff peaks. Spoon the cream into the piping/pastry bag.

Heat the hot chocolate again and carefully pour into two heatproof glasses or cups. Add a cube of Turkish delight to each glass, then pipe a swirl of cream on top of each glass. Finely chopped the remaining Turkish delight and sprinkle over the cream. Add some edible rose petals, if you like. Serve immediately.

Cherry Bakewell hot chocolate

This hot chocolate is inspired by the English bakewell tart - traditionally filled with almond frangipane and cherry jam and topped with a glossy glacé/candied cherry. The white hot chocolate is scented with Amaretto liqueur and almond extract, and topped with whipped cream, cherry syrup and a cherry. This is lovely served as dessert.

100 g/3½ oz. white chocolate, chopped

500 ml/2 cups milk

I teaspoon almond extract

4–5 tablespoons Amaretto liqueur or almond liqueur

150 ml/²/3 cup double/heavy cream

cherry syrup, to drizzle

2 glacé/candied cherries

piping/pastry bag fitted with a large star nozzle/tip

Serves 2

Place the chopped white chocolate in a saucepan with the milk and almond extract. Heat gently over low heat until the chocolate has melted, whisking all the time. Remove the hot chocolate from the heat and add the Amaretto liqueur or almond liqueur (it is best to do this off the heat so that the alcohol does not evaporate too much).

Place the cream in a bowl and whisk to stiff peaks.

Pour the hot chocolate into two cups. Spoon the whipped cream into the piping/pastry bag and pipe a swirl of cream on top of each hot chocolate. Drizzle with a little cherry syrup (take care not to drizzle too much cherry syrup as it can cause the hot chocolate to curdle) and top each with a glacé/candied cherry. Serve immediately.

Toffee apple hot chocolate

Eating toffee apples at Halloween and on Bonfire Night is such a treat - biting into the crisp caramel shell and then finding the juicy apple underneath. This hot chocolate is flavoured with caramelized sugar, and you should take the caramel as dark as you dare (without burning it) to get the maximum caramel flavour in the milk. Apfelkorn liqueur is a tasty German apple spirit which is very warming. It is available online and from good drinks retailers.

1 dessert apple

freshly squeezed juice of ½ lemon

1 teaspoon ground cinnamon

100 g/½ cup caster/superfine sugar

500 ml/2 cups milk

40 g/1½ oz. white chocolate, chopped

4 tablespoons Apfelkorn liqueur (optional)

spray cream or whipped cream, for topping

dulce de leche sauce, to drizzle

silicone mat or baking sheet lined with greaseproof paper

Serves 2

Preheat the oven to 140°C (275°F) Gas 1.

Leaving the skin on, cut the apple into thin slices using a sharp knife or a mandoline. Toss the slices in lemon juice to prevent them browning, then dust in a little ground cinnamon. Lay the slices out flat on a baking sheet and bake in the preheated oven for 1–1½ hours, until dried but still slightly soft. (This will make more dried apple than you need for decoration but they will keep well and make a great healthy snack if stored in an airtight container.)

Place the sugar in a saucepan and heat gently over low heat until melted. Do not stir, but swirl it to ensure that the sugar does not burn. Once the sugar has melted, carefully dip some of the baked apple slices into the caramel — only dipping them in half way. (Use tongs and take extreme care as the sugar is very hot and can burn you.) Place the apple slices on a silicone mat or baking sheet lined with greaseproof paper and leave to dry.

Add the milk to the remaining caramelized sugar in the pan. Do not worry if the sugar solidifies, as it will melt on heating. Simmer over low heat until the sugar dissolves. Add the chocolate and stir until melted. Remove from the heat and add the apfelkorn (do not return to the heat as it may curdle the milk). Pour the hot chocolate into two cups, top with a little whipped cream and drizzle with dulce de leche. Place an apple slice on top of each cup. Serve immediately.

Fireside favourites

Cinnamon and clementine hot chocolate

If there is one flavour that instantly transports me to Christmas day it is the humble clementine as I always find one at the bottom of my Christmas stocking. The bitter chocolate is sweetened with a delicious homemade clementine syrup. If you have spare clementines, increase the syrup quantity and use the extra in prosecco or Champagne for a festive cocktail.

2 tablespoons caster/superfine sugar

grated zest and freshly squeezed juice of 2 clementines

2 long cinnamon sticks

½ teaspoon ground cinnamon

500 ml/2 cups milk

100 g/3½ oz. dark/bittersweet chocolate (85% cocoa solids), chopped

mini marshmallows, to serve

unsweetened cocoa powder, for sprinkling

Serves 2

Begin by making the clementine syrup. Place the sugar and clementine zest and juice in a small saucepan and simmer over low heat until the sugar has dissolved and the liquid is syrupy.

Add the cinnamon sticks and ground cinnamon to the saucepan along with the milk and chopped chocolate. Simmer over low heat until the chocolate has melted, whisking to incorporate the chocolate.

Remove the cinnamon sticks from the pan and rinse them. Pour the hot chocolate into two heatproof glasses or cups and top with a layer of mini marshmallows. Sprinkle with cocoa powder and place a cinnamon stick in each glass to act as a stirrer. Serve immediately.

Cherry brandy hot chocolate

This is a hot chocolate with a grown-up kick - indulgent with cherry brandy and a kitsch maraschino cherry swizzle stick. I'd like to think that if they were to have sipped on hot chocolates in the roaring 1920s, something like this is what they would have enjoyed.

100 g/3½ oz. plain/semisweet chocolate, chopped

1 tablespoon icing/confectioners' sugar

250 ml/1 cup milk

250 ml/1 cup double/heavy cream

5 tablespoons cherry brandy

2 tablespoons cherry pie filling

6 maraschino cherries

spray cream or whipped cream, for serving (optional)

2 small wooden skewers

Serves 2

Place the chopped chocolate in a saucepan with the sugar, milk and cream. Simmer over low heat until the chocolate has melted, whisking all the time. Remove from the heat and add the cherry brandy. (Do not do this over the heat otherwise it will cause the alcohol to evaporate and you will lose some of the boozy flavour.)

Place a tablespoonful of cherry pie filling into the bottom of two heatproof glasses, then carefully pour in the hot chocolate. Thread the cherries onto the wooden skewers (if necessary trim the skewers to a size about 6 cm/2½ inches taller than your glasses).

Place a cherry skewer in each glass to serve. Serve with some whipped cream on the side, if you like, and with spoons, so that once you have drunk the drink you can eat the warm cherries at the bottom of the glass.

Chai-spiced white hot chocolate

Chai tea is a popular Indian drink delicately fragranced with cinnamon and cardamom. The spicing of the tea varies from region to region, and every family's recipe for the chai masala is different. I have used that delicious drink as the inspiration for this white hot chocolate with my favourite spices and a hint of rose water for added perfume. This drink is also nice chilled on ice as a summer white chocolate milkshake.

12 green cardamom pods

1 teaspoon caster/superfine sugar

1 cinnamon stick

a pinch of freshly grated nutmeg, plus extra to serve

500 ml/2 cups milk

1 teaspoon rose extract, water or syrup

100 g/3½ oz. white chocolate, chopped

pestle and mortar

Serves 2

Begin by removing the black seeds from two of the cardamom pods and grinding them to a fine powder with the sugar using a pestle and mortar.

Place the ground cardamom and remaining pods in a saucepan with the cinnamon stick, nutmeg and milk, and bring to the boil over low heat. Remove from the heat and leave the spices to infuse for 15–20 minutes, then discard the whole pods and cinnamon stick.

Add the rose extract and chopped white chocolate to the pan and return to a simmer over low heat, whisking all the time, until the chocolate has melted. Pour into two cups or heatproof glasses and serve immediately, sprinkled with extra freshly grated nutmeg, if you like.

Irish dream

When it is cold, Irish Cream liqueurs are perfect for warming the soul, and what better way to do this than by flavouring hot chocolate with this delicious whiskey-based drink. This rich and luxurious hot chocolate is topped with whipped caramel cream and curls of white chocolate, making it one very naughty tipple.

100 g/3½ oz. bar of white chocolate

450 ml/scant 2 cups double/heavy cream

250 ml/1 cup milk

100 ml/⅓ cup Baileys or other cream liqueur

1 tablespoon caramel sauce, plus extra to drizzle

swivel peeler or box grater

Serves 2

Pull the swivel peeler along one of the long edges of the white chocolate bar to make a few ribbons of chocolate. It is best to do this with the chocolate at room temperature rather than chilled, so that it doesn't break. You just need a few chocolate curls to top each hot chocolate as decoration. Keep the chocolate curls in the refrigerator until you are ready to serve. Alternatively, simply grate some chocolate instead.

Chop the remaining chocolate into chunks and place in a saucepan with 250 ml/1 cup of the cream and the milk. Simmer over low heat until the chocolate has melted, whisking all the time. Remove from the heat and add the Baileys or cream liqueur. (Do not do this over the heat otherwise it will cause the alcohol to evaporate — definitely not something I would recommend!)

Place the remaining cream in a mixing bowl with the caramel sauce and whisk to stiff peaks. Pour the hot chocolate into two cups or heatproof glasses and spoon some caramel cream on top. Drizzle with a little extra caramel sauce, if you wish, and top with the chocolate curls. Serve immediately.

La bomba

If there is one drink that transports me to my younger years, it is this one. My wonderful Grandparents, Dennis and Marjorie, used to go on holiday to Camp de Mar in Mallorca every single year. They stayed in the same hotel 17 times and everyone there knew them well. Evenings would be spent at Pepe's bar drinking this wonderful rum-flavoured hot chocolate – La bomba – happy days! Serve with churros (Spanish doughnuts), if you wish.

100 g/3½ oz. plain/semisweet chocolate, chopped

1 tablespoon icing/confectioners' sugar

500 ml/2 cups milk

200 ml/generous ¾ cup double/heavy cream

2 tablespoons rum, plus 2 shots to serve

piping/pastry bag fitted with a large star nozzle/tip

2 shot glasses

Serves 2

Place the chopped chocolate in a saucepan with the sugar and milk and simmer over low heat until the chocolate has melted, whisking all the time.

Place the cream in a mixing bowl with the 2 tablespoons rum and whisk to stiff peaks. Spoon the rum cream into the piping/pastry bag.

Pour the hot chocolate into two cups or heatproof glasses and pipe a large swirl of rum cream on top of each. (Do not fill to the very top as you need to leave room for the rum to be added.)

Serve the hot chocolate immediately with a shot of rum on the side. To drink, pour the rum into the hot chocolate and enjoy.

Maple pecan bourbon hot chocolate

This is proper grown-up hot chocolate – manly hot chocolate if you will! Laced with bourbon whiskey and maple syrup, it warms you to the core. It is a great drink for adults to take out in a flask for cold winter walks.

50 g/¼ cup caster/superfine sugar

3 tablespoons pecan halves

100 g/3½ oz. milk chocolate, chopped

250 ml/1 cup double/heavy cream

250 ml/1 cup milk

100 ml/⅓ cup maple syrup

1 teaspoon vanilla bean paste or pure vanilla extract

100 ml/⅓ cup bourbon whiskey

silicone mat or greased baking sheet

food processor or blender

Serves 2

For the pecan praline, heat the sugar in a saucepan until it melts, swirling the pan to prevent the sugar from burning. Do not stir with a spoon. You need to watch very carefully because it can burn very easily. Once the sugar is a golden caramel colour, spread the pecans out on a silicone mat or greased baking sheet, and then pour over the melted sugar. Leave to cool, then blitz to fine crumbs in a food processor or blender. Place the praline powder on a plate.

Next prepare two heatproof glasses. Place the chopped chocolate in a heatproof bowl over a pan of simmering water and heat over low heat until melted. Carefully dip the rim of each glass into the melted chocolate, then roll the edge of the rim of each chocolate-coated glass in the praline to decorate. Set aside until you are ready to serve.

Spoon the remaining melted chocolate into a saucepan and add the cream, milk, maple syrup, vanilla and bourbon, and simmer over low heat until combined, whisking all the time. Pour the hot chocolate into the prepared glasses, taking care not to pour it over the chocolate-praline decoration. Serve immediately.

Hazelnut hot chocolate

This drink is a must for all Nutella lovers - rich and creamy with a hit of hazelnut liqueur. Sprinkled with hazelnuts, this is an utterly nutterly hot chocolate. Top with half a Ferrero Rocher for an extra-special treat. If you are making this for children, it is equally delicious without the alcohol.

100 g/3½ oz. milk chocolate, chopped

500 ml/2 cups milk

1 heaped tablespoon chocolate hazelnut spread (such as Nutella)

4–7 tablespoons hazelnut liqueur (such as Frangelico)

200 ml/generous ¾ cup double/heavy cream

1 tablespoon finely chopped hazelnuts, toasted

1 Ferrero Rocher chocolate, halved (optional)

Serves 2

Place the chopped chocolate in a heatproof bowl over a pan of simmering water and heat gently over low heat until melted.

Place the milk in a saucepan and bring gently to the boil. Add the melted chocolate and Nutella to the pan and simmer over low heat, whisking all the time, until the chocolate is combined. Remove from the heat and add the hazelnut liqueur to taste. (Do not do this over the heat as the alcohol will evaporate.)

Pour the hot chocolate into two cups.

Whip the cream to stiff peaks and add a spoonful to the top of each serving. Sprinkle with toasted hazelnuts. Add a Ferrero Rocher half to each serving too, if you wish. Serve immediately.

Chilli hot chocolate

Chilli/chile and chocolate may seem a fiery combination, but fear not, this chocolate is not too hot. The chilli/chile gives a depth of flavour to the bitter chocolate. If you want, you can make extra candied chillies/chiles to serve with your hot chocolate for the brave, although poaching them in sugar syrup does take away a lot of the heat.

100 g/½ cup caster/granulated sugar

1–5 fresh large red chillies/chiles

200 ml/generous ¾ cup milk

100 ml/⅓ cup double/heavy cream

100 g/3½ oz. dark/bittersweet chilli/chile chocolate, chopped

Serves 2

Begin by preparing the candied chillies. Place the sugar in a saucepan with 250 ml/I cup water and simmer over medium heat until the sugar has dissolved. Add the chillies/chiles (with their green tops still attached) to the pan and simmer for 15–20 minutes, until the chillies/chiles are soft and their skins are slightly translucent. Remove the chillies/chiles from the pan and reserve I tablespoon of the poaching syrup. Set aside.

Place the milk, cream and chopped chocolate in a saucepan and heat over low heat until the chocolate has melted, whisking all the time.

Finely chop one of the candied chillies/chiles and add a little of the chopped chilli/chile to the pan, together with the reserved syrup. (How much you add depends on your own taste and the strength of your chillies/chiles. Add a little to start, then taste and add more if you want a more fiery flavour.)

Pour the hot chocolate into two cups and serve straight away with extra candied chillies/chiles on the side, if you wish.

Festive treats

White chocolate eggnog

My friend Lucy loves eggnog - such an old-fashioned drink but a truly festive one. This is my hot chocolate version which I love to make for Lucy at Christmas and serve with classic German iced gingerbread lebkuchen.

3 egg yolks

2 tablespoons caster/superfine sugar

500 ml/2 cups milk

100 g/3½ oz. white chocolate, chopped

1 teaspoon ground cinnamon

a pinch of freshly grated nutmeg

1 teaspoon vanilla bean paste or pure vanilla extract

4–5 tablespoons rum (or more if you prefer!)

Serves 2

In a large mixing bowl, whisk together the egg yolks and sugar until thick and creamy. Set aside.

Place the milk and chopped white chocolate in a saucepan with the cinnamon, nutmeg and vanilla, and heat over low heat until the chocolate has melted, whisking all the time.

Bring the milk mixture gently to the boil and then pour over the egg yolk mixture, whisking all the time. (It is easiest to ask someone to whisk for you while you pour the hot milk in). Return the mixture to the pan and simmer over low heat until the drink starts to thicken, whisking continuously, then remove from the heat and stir in the rum.

Serve immediately in heatproof glasses or alternatively you can cool, then chill this drink and serve cold for equally delicious results.

Gingerbread-spiced hot chocolate

I love the flavour of ginger, and gingerbread hot chocolate is one of my favourites. You can make this hot chocolate with milk, plain/semisweet, dark/bittersweet or white chocolate and they are all equally delicious. Flavoured with stem ginger and gingerbread syrup, this is the perfect drink to sip by the fireside. For an extra treat, serve with gingerbread cookies on the side. If you do not have gingerbread syrup, simply double the quantity of ginger syrup used and add a little ground cinnamon and a pinch of freshly grated nutmeg to the milk.

100 g/3½ oz. milk chocolate, chopped

500 ml/2 cups milk

1 ball preserved stem ginger and 1 tablespoon ginger syrup from the jar

1 tablespoon gingerbread syrup

spray cream or whipped cream, for topping

gingerbread man sprinkles, to decorate

Serves 2

Place the chopped chocolate in a saucepan with the milk, stem ginger, ginger syrup and gingerbread syrup. Simmer over low heat until the chocolate has melted, whisking all the time.

Remove the stem ginger and discard. Pour the hot chocolate into two cups and top with cream. Decorate with gingerbread man sprinkles and serve immediately.

Pumpkin latte

I often spend holidays in New York where my brother lives, and while there, I like to share the American passion for the humble pumpkin. I love pumpkin pie, pumpkin muffins and even pumpkin purée in coffee, so this recipe was a no-brainer for inclusion in this book. This drink is perfect to serve for Halloween and Thanksgiving celebrations.

2 tablespoons pumpkin purée (such as Libby's)

100 g/3½ oz. white chocolate, chopped

500 ml/2 cups milk

a pinch of freshly grated nutmeg, plus extra to decorate

1 teaspoon ground cinnamon

½ teaspoon ground ginger

1 teaspoon pure vanilla extract

spray cream or whipped cream, for topping

blender (optional)

Serves 2

Place the pumpkin purée and chopped white chocolate in a saucepan with the milk, nutmeg, cinnamon, ginger and vanilla. Simmer over low heat until the chocolate has melted, whisking all the time. For an extra-smooth hot chocolate, place the mixture in a blender now and blitz for a few seconds. This is optional though, as I also enjoy the drink with the slight texture of the purée.

Return the hot chocolate to the pan if necessary, and heat again, then pour into two heatproof glasses or cups to serve. Top with cream and finish with an extra pinch of grated nutmeg. Serve immediately.

Peppermint candy cane hot chocolate

I always hang candy canes on my tree at Christmas and they make the perfect swizzle stick for this festive hot chocolate. To make your glasses extra special, dip the tops in melted white chocolate and decorate the rims with crushed candy canes as well. This hot chocolate is made with chocolate-coated mint fondants, such as After Eights, although you could substitute peppermint-flavoured dark/bitterweet chocolate, if you prefer. For a white chocolate version, use white chocolate and a teaspoon of peppermint extract or white chocolate-coated mint fondants, if you can find them.

50 g/2 oz. white chocolate, chopped

4 candy canes

100 g/3½ oz. chocolate-coated mint fondants (such as After Eights)

250 ml/1 cup milk

450 ml/scant 2 cups double/heavy cream

Serves 2

Begin by preparing the glasses. Place the white chocolate in a heatproof bowl over a pan of simmering water and heat until melted. Carefully dip the rims of two heatproof glasses into the chocolate. Crush two of the candy canes into small pieces by placing them in a clean plastic bag and bashing them with a rolling pin. Place the peppermint pieces on a plate and roll the edge of the rim of each chocolate-coated glass in the peppermint pieces to decorate. Set aside, reserving any leftover mint pieces for decoration.

Place the chocolate-coated mint fondants in a saucepan with the milk and 250 ml/1 cup of the cream and bring to the boil over low heat, whisking all the time. Pour the hot chocolate into the prepared glasses, taking care not to pour it over the decorated rims.

Whip the remaining cream to stiff peaks and place a large spoonful on top of each drink. Sprinkle with any leftover peppermint pieces and place a whole candy cane in each glass to serve. Serve immediately.

Orange dream hot chocolate

Every Christmas I get a Terry's Chocolate Orange in my stocking, so sipping this hot chocolate tastes to me of Christmas morning. For an extra-special treat, I top this drink with homemade orange marshmallows - not too tricky to prepare and they make the perfect gooey topping for this delicious drink. They are also perfect to give as gifts.

freshly squeezed juice of 2 oranges

2 tablespoons caster/superfine sugar

500 ml/2 cups milk

100 g/3½ oz. orange-flavoured dark/bittersweet chocolate (or plain dark/bittersweet chocolate), chopped

4 tablespoons Grand Marnier or other orange liqueur (optional)

FOR THE MARSHMALLOWS

200 ml/generous ¾ cup freshly squeezed orange juice and grated zest of 1 orange

4 teaspoons powdered gelatine

250 g/1¼ cups caster/superfine sugar

2 tablespoons liquid glucose

orange food colouring

icing/confectioners' sugar, sifted, for dusting

sugar thermometer

roasting pan lined with clingfilm/plastic wrap or a silicone mat

Begin by making the marshmallows as they need to set before being used. Whisk together 5 tablespoons of the orange juice and the powdered gelatine in a large mixing bowl. (For best results use a stand mixer because you will need to whisk the mixture a lot later.) Place the sugar, glucose and remaining 125 ml/½ cup orange juice and the zest into a heavy-based pan and simmer over low heat until the sugar has dissolved. Turn up the heat and boil the mixture until it reaches hardball stage on a sugar thermometer (128°C/263°F). Turn the stand mixer on and, whisking constantly, pour the hot syrup over the gelatine mixture in a thin, steady stream and whisk for about 10 minutes, until the mixture becomes white, thick and meringue-like. Whisk in a few drops of orange food colouring.

Dust the lined roasting pan with a thin layer of icing/confectioners' sugar. Pour the marshmallow mixture into the prepared pan. Dust the top with more icing/confectioners' sugar and leave to set for 2 hours in the refrigerator.

Turn the marshmallow out onto a flat surface and gently remove the clingfilm/plastic wrap. Dust with more icing/confectioners' sugar. Cut the marshmallow into squares. Store in an airtight container for up to 1 week.

For the hot chocolate, simmer the orange juice and sugar in a saucepan over low heat until the sugar has melted and you have a sticky syrup. Add the milk and chocolate, and heat gently until the chocolate has melted, whisking all the time. Remove from the heat and add the Grand Marnier, if using. Stir, then pour into cups. Top with a few orange marshmallows and serve immediately. If you do not have time to make homemade marshmallows, substitute with store-bought ones instead.

Serves 2

Index